After Semyon Izrailevich Lipkin

Acknowledgments

Some of the translations have been published in *The Assay* (2010), *Cardinal Points, The Manchester Review* and *Poetry Review*.

After Semyon Izrailevich Lipkin
Yvonne Green

Smith/Doorstop Books

Published 2011 by
Smith/Doorstop Books
The Poetry Business
Bank Street Arts
32-40 Bank Street
Sheffield S1 2DS
www.poetrybusiness.co.uk

ISBN 978-1-906613-38-9

British Library Cataloguing-in-Publication Data.
A catalogue record for this book is available from the
British Library.

Typeset by Utter
Printed by Charlesworth, Wakefield
Cover design by Utter

Smith/Doorstop Books is a member of Inpress,
www.inpressbooks.co.uk. Distributed by Central Books Ltd.,
99 Wallis Road, London E9 5LN.

The Poetry Business gratefully acknowledges the help of
Arts Council England.

Supported by
**ARTS COUNCIL
ENGLAND**

Contents

Poems After Semyon Izrailevich Lipkin

Appendix

To Inna, Lena and Sergei

Introduction by Yvonne Green

I read Inna Lisnianskaya's poetry in the translation *Far From Sodom* (Daniel Weissbort, Arc Publications, 2005) and loved its perception, in particular the glimpses of her late husband, Semyon Lipkin's, insight.

Only a handful of Lipkin's poems had been translated, so by audio taping Russian friends reading them, and using literal translations obtained word by word, line by line and by examining the evident patchwork of rhyme visible on the page and with the help of a phonetic copy of the Cyrillic alphabet I began my search to understand Lipkin's poems, and bring them to an English reader.

The project has taken six years. I'm indebted to many people along the road. I'd like to start by thanking Fiona Sampson, editor of *Poetry Review*, for publishing my first efforts, which proved a great encouragement.

Lipkin's work was informed by three sources, his personal experience of war (he served at Stalingrad), his friend Vasily Grossman's reports of Treblinka, and his encyclopedic knowledge of the languages and history of Central Asia. He translated from Buriat, Dagestani, Farsi, Kalmyk, Kabardian, Kirghiz, Tatar, Tadjik and Uzbek.

Lipkin preserved cultures that Sovietisation undermined by translating their poetry into Russian. These included versions of the Kalmyk epic *Dzhangar* (1940), the Kirghiz epic *Manas* (1941), the Kabardian epic *Narty* (1951), the Buriat epic *Geser* (1968), and the classic works of the classical Tadzhik, Uzbek, Kirghiz, Balkar and Kalmyk poets. His translations were published as *Kabardian Epic Poetry* (1956), *Voices of Six Centuries* (1960), and *The Golden Chain: Eastern Poems* (1970). Lipkin received prizes detailed in the Chronology of this book as well as four orders and a number of medals.

He was not alone amongst his beleaguered compatriots, some of whom also translated when their poems were banned; but his work was recognized by Tsvetaeva and Brodsky to have been unique. They singled out his own poetry beyond his generous oeuvre of translation, which until Perestroika was read in manuscript or heard recited from memory by very few.

Lipkin's son-in-law, Sergei Makarov said to me, "Lipkin knew about everything, politics, economics, culture, religion". Inna, said slicing the air above her head with her slim, vermillion manicured, hand, "he loved people who loved God". Which I took to mean, who understood they weren't supreme.

If my translations succeed in no other respect I hope they show how Lipkin recognized supremacism and loathed it.

Robert and Elizabeth Chandler, Peter Daniels, Masha Karp, Ruth Padel and Sharon Dewinter each helped or encouraged me to fledge this book. Inna Lisnianskaya and her daughter Lena Makarova gave me generous and patient support from the outset. Lena works tirelessly documenting the thousands of lectures, plays, operas, concerts, and works of fine art produced at Tereizen by inmates who went on to their deaths. Every moment she gave me was beyond value.

There are many theories about how translation should be approached; Nabokov's line by line with footnotes; Brodsky's insistence that rhyme and meter be reproduced faithfully; Hughes' assertion that translation should not be smooth; the current fashion for intuited translation. 'Moldavian is a Language' at page 36 of this book is an example of an attempt I made to mimic form, in 'Anthem' at page 25, I used hyphenated words to counteract smoothness, but on the whole I've tried to convey the internal conversation of Lipkin's work. Any failures are my own and not those of my co-translators.

My hope is that other writers will make their own versions of Lipkin's supremely classical poems. His use of form and language is matchless. Lipkin lived an extraordinary life through extraordinary times and wrote the poems I've translated here about those events listed in the Chronology.. In addition, it was he who saved Vasily Grossman's manuscript of *Life and Fate* from the KGB and took further personal risks to set it on course for publication in the West eleven years after Grossman's death. He is a poet revered throughout the former USSR but virtually unknown in the West.

Chronology

1911, September 6 (Julian Calendar)
Semyon Izrailevich Lipkin born 19 September (Gregorian
Calendar), 1911, Odessa; son of Israel and Rosalia Lipkin; his
father had a tailoring business.

1914, June 28
Franz Ferdinand, Archduke of Austria and his wife are
assassinated in Sarajevo by Gavrilo Princip, the *casus belli* of the
First World War.

1917   Bolshevik revolution.

1918–20   Civil war

1921–22   Famine in Volga basin

1924   Death of Lenin. Petrograd is renamed Leningrad. Stalin begins
to take over power.

1925   Lipkin's first poem published, age 15. Eduard Bagritskii
recognises the merit of this first publication.

1930, February
Central Committee Decree calls for the liquidation of the
Kulaks as a class.

April 14
Mayakovsky commits suicide.

1931   Stalin orders enforced collectivization. Kalmyk Buddhist
monasteries closed, and religious texts burned.

1932   Central Committee issues decree on the reconstruction of
Literary-Artistic organisations.

1932–33   Between 3,000,000 and 5,000,000 peasants killed by their own
government's Terror Famine (Holodomor) in the Ukraine and
approximately 4,000,000 elsewhere in the Soviet Union (of
which 60,000 are Kalmyks).

1934   Union of Soviet Writers formed.

1936   Stalin denounces Shostakovich's Lady Macbeth of Mtsensk.

1936–38   Approximately half the members of the Soviet political, military and intellectual elite are imprisoned or shot. Around 380,000 supposed 'Kulaks' are killed, as are around 250,000 members of various national minorities.

1937   Lipkin graduates from the Moscow Economics Engineering Institute. While studying engineering he had begun studying Farsi, followed by other oriental languages including Dagestani, Kalmyk, Kirgiz, Tatar, Tadjik, Uzbek, Kabardin, Yiddish and Moldavian; also their history and culture including Islam and Buddhism.

1939–41   Death of 70,000 handicapped Germans in the Nazis' euthanasia programme.

1939   Nazi–Soviet pact. Beginning of Second World War.

1941   Lipkin's friend Vasily Grossman, starts work as a war correspondent for The Red Army's newspaper.

June 22
Germany invades the Soviet Union.

August
Leningrad is blockaded.

September 8
Siege of Leningrad begins.

October
Moscow is under threat.

1941–42   Nazis shoot an estimated 2,000,000 Jews in western USSR, Grossman's mother killed along with approximately 12,000 in a day at the airport outside Berdichev.

1941–44   2,500,000 Jews are gassed in Poland at Chelmno, Majdanek, Belzec, Sobibor, Treblinka and Auschwitz.

1941–45   Lipkin served in the Red Army, including at Stalingrad.

1942–1943, August to February
Battle of Stalingrad.

1943, January
Soviets reconquer the Kalmyk ASSR.

1943, July/August
Decisive Soviet victories at Kursk, Orel and Kharkov.

1943   Stalin declares all Kalmyks to be Nazi collaborators. In December the total population of the Kalmyk ASSR, including communists, is deported to prison camps in Siberia and Central Asia.

1944, January 27
Siege of Leningrad lifted.

April–June
436,000 Hungarian Jews are gassed at Auschwitz in 56 days.

August-October
The Warsaw Uprising.

1945, January 27
Liberation of Auschwitz.

May 8
Germany surrenders.

1946   Nuremberg Trial of the Nazi leadership. In the Soviet Union, Andrey Zhdanov tightens control over the arts.

1948   Murder of Mikhoels, head of the Jewish Anti-Fascist Committee which was then dissolved. The plates for the Soviet edition of *The Black Book*, a documentary of the Final Solution in the Soviet Union and Poland, compiled by Ilya Ehrenburg and Grossman between 1943-1946 are destroyed.

1953, January
Article in Pravda about the Jewish "Killer Doctors", purge of USSR's Jews being planned

March 5
Stalin dies.

April 4
Officials acknowledge "Killer Doctors" claim a fabrication

1956, February
Khrushchev's Secret Speech to the Communist Party. He denounces the forcible exile of the Kalmyks, Karachai, Chechen, Ingush, and Balkhars.

1956, Oct–Nov
Suppression of Hungarian insurrection.

1957   Some Kalmyks allowed to return. Pasternak's Dr. Zhivago is published in Italy.

1958   The former Kalmyk ASSR reconstituted. Under pressure from
          the Soviet authorities Pasternak declines the Nobel Prize.

1960 October
          Against the advice of Yekaterina Vasilievna Zabolotskaya and
          Lipkin, Vasily Grossman submits his novel *Life and Fate* for
          publication to the editors of *Znamya*.

1961   The KGB raid Grossman's home and destroy all the copies of
          Life and Fate they can. Lipkin keeps one copy at Peredelkino and
          later transfers it to Sergei and Lena Makarov's attic in Moscow
          for safe keeping. Unbeknown to Lipkin, Lyola Klestova has been
          given the original manuscript by Grossman who arranges prior
          to his death for her to give her copy to Vyacheslav Loboda.

1962, November
          Alexander Solzhenitsyn's *One Day in the Life of Ivan Denisovich*
          published in the Soviet Union.

1964   Fall of Khrushchev; death of Vasily Grossman.

1966   Trial of Sinyavski and Daniel.

1967   Lipkin receives the Rudaki State Prize of the Tadzhik SSR.
          Lipkin's first collection of poetry *Ochevidets [Eyewitness]*
          published. His poem 'Conjunction' is read as coded support for
          Israel.

1968, August
          Warsaw Pact invasion of Czechoslovakia.

1968   Lipkin made People's Poet of the Kalmyk ASSR.

1970   First issue of Jewish samizdat journal *Exodus*. Lipkin's *A
          Notebook of Being* published.

1971   Beginning of permitted Jewish emigration.

1973   The first parts of Solzhenitsyn's *Gulag Archipelago* published in
          Paris.

1974   Solzhenitsyn, having been charged and found guilty of treason,
          exiled from the USSR.

1975   Sakharov awarded Nobel Peace Prize. Lipkin's *Vechnyi Den'
          [Eternal Day]* published. Lipkin asks the writer Vladimir
          Voinovich to help him get his copy of *Life and Fate* (the

manuscript) published in the West. Voinovich inexpertly microfilms the manuscript but then gets Andrey Sakharov to make a better microfilm. The latter film reaches the Parisian dissident journal *Kontinent* via Russia's Austrian Attaché. Only extracts are published.

1977   Voinovich microfilms the manuscript again and it reaches Yefim Etkind and Shimon Markish via the Austrian Professor Rosemary Zeigler.

1979   Lipkin and Inna Lisnyanskaya submit their poetry to the anthology *Metropol,* which is rejected by the Soviet authorities.

1980   Lipkin resigns from the Union of Writers. Internal exile of Sakharov. Grossman's *Life and Fate* published in Switzerland, from Voinovich's films of the manuscript as painstakingly collated by Etkind and Markish.

1981   *Metropol* published in the United States. Lipkin's *Volya* [Free Will] published in Russian in the US on the iniative of Joseph Brodsky.

1982, November 10
        Brezhnev dies.

1984   Death of Andropov. Lipkin's *Kochevoi Ogon' [A Nomadic Flame]* published in Russian in US.

1985   Gorbachev becomes general secretary of the Communist Party of the Soviet Union. The period known as perestroika begins. Loboda's widow shows the original manuscript of *Life and Fate* to Fyodor Guber and it was used to correct textual lacunae in the Swiss version before *Life and Fate* was first published in Moscow. The first publication in Russia of *Life and Fate* along with Grossman's *Everything Flows* and important works by Krzhizhanovsky, Platonov, Shalamov, Solzhenitsyn and many others.

1986   Lipkin's *Kartiny i golosa [Pictures and Voices]* published in Russian in London, he is reinstated into The Writers' Union.

1988   Pasternak's *Doctor Zhivago* published in Soviet Union. October: Gorbachev becomes Head of State.

1989, November
        Fall of Berlin Wall.

1991	Dissolution of USSR. Lipkin awarded Tukai Prize. His *Lunnyi Svet [Moonlight]* and *Pis'mena [Letters]* published.
1992/93	Outbreak of civil war in Tajikistan.
1993	Yeltsin suppresses armed rising by Supreme Soviet.
1995	Lipkin awarded the Sakharov Prize by the European Parliament, and the Pushkin Prize by the Alfred Toepfer Foundation, Germany.
1997	Lipkin's *Posokh [Shepherd's Crook]* published.
2000	Putin elected president. Lipkin's *Sem' desiatiletii [Seven Decades]* published.
2003, May 31	Death of Semyon Izrailevich Lipkin at Peredelkino.

Literal Translations by:

Olga Selivanova (OS)

Sveta Payne (SP)

Sergei Makarov (SM)

Mariya Petrova (MP)

Where no co-translator is named my literal was provided by a translator who did not wish to be credited.

Poems After Semyon Izrailevich Lipkin

Зола

Я был остывшею золой
Без мысли, облика и речи,
Но вышел я на путь земной
Из чрева матери — из печи.

Еще и жизни не поняв
И прежней смерти не оплакав,
Я шел среди баварских трав
И обезлюдевших бараков.

Неспешно в сумерках текли
«Фольксвагены» и «мерседесы»,
А я шептал: «Меня сожгли.
Как мне добраться до Одессы?»

(1967)

Charred

and ashen I whisper *I've been cremated*
in deserted barracks on Bavarian grasslands.

I think *I'm blind confounded*
my palate has claimed my tongue.

When Mercedes Benz' and Volkswagens
course silently through evening autobahns

I ask *how do I find my way to Odessa?*
Born burnt I can't yet mourn

what it means to be alive or dead.
My cold embers won't light a flame

(After 'Ashes')

[SP and YG]

Инне

Раскольничьи твои слова грустят,
То яростью сжигаясь, то стыдом,
И сумрачно твои глаза блестят —
Два зеркала, облитые дождём.

И в этом жарком, влажном пепле глаз,
Столь соприродных мирозданьям двум,
Открыл я бред и боль двух древних рас,
Души дремотной бодрствующий ум.

(1979)

To Inna

Burdened with sadness
you speak your beliefs
whatever it costs you.
Frenzied then guilty
your eyes deaden
like unsilvered mirror

burn with the hot moist ash
of two histories, show
two ancient races'
pain and terror.
In them I've seen
the taut mind
of a deep soul

[SP and YG]

Военная Песня

Что ты заводишь песню военну.
Державин

Серое небо. Травы сырые.
В яме икона панны Марии.
Враг отступает. Мы победили.
Думать не надо. Плакать нельзя.
Мертвый ягненок. Мертвые хаты.
Между развалин — наши солдаты.
В лагере пусто. Печи остыли.
Думать не надо. Плакать нельзя.

Страшно, ей-богу, там, за фольварком.
Хлопцы, разлейте старку по чаркам,
Скоро в дорогу. Скоро награда.
А до парада плакать нельзя.
Черные печи да мыловарни.
Здесь потрудились прусские парни.
Где эти парни? Думать не надо.
Мы победили. Плакать нельзя.

В полураскрытом чреве вагона —
Детское тельце. Круг патефона.
Видимо, ветер вертит пластинку.
Слушать нет силы. Плакать нельзя.
В лагере смерти печи остыли.
Крутится песня. Мы победили.
Мама, закутай дочку в простынку.
Пой, балалайка, плакать нельзя.

(1981)

Anthem

Derzhavin, your anthem has no place here
under ashy sky, on pulped grass.
The Virgin's icon lies splintered,
in a pit of lime, as the enemy leaves us
to our confounded blink-eyed victory.
Lamb-dead, hut-vacant, camp-silent,
soldier-furrowed, soap-charred.
Almighty, I'm afraid to go beyond the fields
vodka-glassed, victory-paraded
strong-man medalled.

A pregnant train is trailing its child.
I can't listen to an anthem gramophoned
by the wind. Mothers must make swaddling
for their girls, the balalaika must sing to me.

(After 'Military Song')

[SP and YG]

25

Моисей

Тропою концентрационной,
Где ночь бессонна, как тюрьма,
Трубой канализационной,
Среди помоев и дерьма,

По всем немецким, и советским,
И польским, и иным путям,
По всем печам, по всем мертвецким,
По всем страстям, по всем смертям, —

Я шел. И грозен и духовен
Впервые Бог открылся мне,
Пылая пламенем газовен
В неопалимой купине.

(1967)

Moses

The train of my black thought
tunnels through heaving sewers
races along all German, Soviet,
Polish roads and beyond.
Hurls through ovens, mortuaries,
ravages. All manner of death.

Then for the first time
God reveals his face to me
intact, spiritual, lit by the blaze
of gas inside the burning bush.

[SP and YG]

Брат

Куда звонить? Конечно, в сад,
Где те же яблоки висят,
Что в тот злосчастный день висели,
Но там и телефона нет,
И никакого звона нет,
И нет печали и веселий.

А он спокойный, не больной,
Оттуда говорит со мной.
Он мальчик. Солнцем жизнь согрета,
А мы бедны, мы босиком
Идем на ближний пляж вдвоем.
Звенит трамвай, пылает лето.

(1996)

Mikhael

Can I call you in the garden
which hasn't changed since
that awful day? The same apples
ripen in the same endless sunshine.
But there's no 'phone to ring
and nothing's left of us there
no laughter, no tears.
When I hear you speak to me now
you've not yet been ill, you're calm,
we're those penniless boys
who cross barefoot to the beach
as passing trams jangle by.

(After 'Brother')

[SP and YG]

Казачка

Сверкает крыша школы, как наждак.
Облиты месяцем арбузы в травке.
Подобно самолету при заправке,
Дрожит большими крыльями ветряк.

Шитье отбросив (на столе - булавки),
То в зеркало глядит, то в полумрак.
Далёко, под Воронежем, казак.
Убит или в больнице на поправке?

Давно нет писем. Комиссар, чудак,
Бормочет что-то о плохой доставке.
Он пристает - и неумело так.

Вошла свекровь. Ее глаза - пиявки.
О, помоги же, месяц в небесах,
Любить, забыться, изойти в слезах!

(1955)

The Cossack Wife

The school roof shines like mica
moonlight soaks watermelons in the young grass
windmill sails drone like jet engines.

A Cossack wife abandons her sewing to the dusk
pins lie on the table, she stares at her mirror:
Is he being nursed or buried now?
It's been so long since he wrote from Voronezh.
The Commissar mumbles that the mail's delayed
then makes his clumsy pass at her.

Her leech eyed mother-in-law lets herself in.
Oh please, full moon in the sky
help the Cossack wife to love, to accept,
to waste herself in tears.

[SP and YG]

Заложник

От Москвы километров отъехали на сто,
И тогда мимо нас, как-то царственно вкось,
Властелин-вавилонянин с телом гимнаста,
Пробежал по тропинке породистый лось.

Князь быков, жрец верховный коровьего стада,
Горбоносый заложник плебея-врага,
От людей не отвел он бесслезного взгляда,
И как знак звездочета темнели рога.

Он боялся машин и дорожного шума,
Как мужчины порою боятся мышей,
Был испуг маловажен, а важная дума
В нем светилась печальною сутью вещей.

Побежать, пожевать бы кипрей узколистный,
А свобода - в созвездиях над головой!
Пленник мира, на мир он смотрел ненавистный,
На союз пожирателей плоти живой.

(1969)

Stopped

Suddenly there's an elk caught
in our headlights. His dry gaze steady
his massive proportions overbearing
his antlers giant like a shaman.

He is thoughtful, not afraid, knowing,
not bemused. We're stopped on this forest path
100 kilometres from Moscow face to face
with the sadness in those eyes.

I wish he'd escape and graze in darkness
let the starlight pierce the black coal of his stare
but instead he stands transfixed by men
who cut the flesh they eat from live animals.

(After 'Hostage')

[SP and YG]

Молдавский язык

Степь шумит, приближаясь к ночлегу,
Загоняя закат за курган,
И тяжелую тащит телегу
Ломовая латынь молдаван.

Слышишь медных глаголов дрожанье?
Это римские речи звучат.
Сотворили-то их каторжане,
А не гордый и грозный сенат.

Отгремел, отблистал Капитолий,
И не стало победных святынь,
Только ветер днестровских раздолий
Ломовую гоняет латынь.

Точно так же блатная музы́ка,
Со словесной порвав чистотой,
Сочиняется вольно и дико
В стане варваров за Воркутой.

За последнюю ложку баланды,
За окурок от чьих-то щедрот
Представителям каторжной банды
Политический что-то поет.

Он поет, этот новый Овидий,
Гениальный болтун-чародей,
О бессмысленном апартеиде
В резервацьи воров и блядей.

Что мы знаем, поющие в бездне,
О грядущем своем далеке?
Будут изданы речи и песни
На когда-то блатном языке.

Ах, Господь, я прочел твою книгу,
И недаром теперь мне дано
На рассвете доесть мамалыгу
И допить молодое вино.

(1962)

Moldavian is a Language

which hauls in the dark
until the last of sunset's banished
by its rugged horse and cart.

Can you hear the swagger,
of its coppery verbs
the Latin of a convict's dagger
not the Senate's words?

The Capitol's heights have crumbled
its artefacts lie low
only the Dniester's windblown grumble
keeps the Roman known.

The songs of desperate outlaws
snipe at the words of the ruler
clatter once they've stopped their chores
at night beyond the Vorkuta.

To earn a bit more dinner
a puff of a cigarette,
the shivering political sinner
is singing aloud and yet

his Ovid is adapted here
crude but still astute
don't segregate yourselves
for fear of thief or prostitute,

desperation makes us equal
as we sing and speak
we each contain the sequel
to the other's pique.

Mamalyga and wine at dawn
give courage to my gullet
and my words are more than brawn
as short lived as a bullet.

One day you'll all be literature
I've read The Almighty's Book
that's why I had to come here
to know to listen to look

[SP and YG]

В Голубом Сосуде

В лесу июля, в голубом сосуде,
Подробно, точно вычерчены ели,
И только люди потому и люди,
Что их угадываешь еле-еле.

Как хорошо, что был Творец неловок,
Что не был увлечен задачей мелкой
И свой небрежный, свежий подмалевок
Он не испортил тщательной отделкой.

(1971)

On a Blue Vase

there's a July forest
with pines drawn in detail
and people in vague silhouette.

Thank God for the impetus
of this imprecise sketch
so brilliantly incomplete

[SP and YG]

Путь

Я шел дорогою безвестной,
Ничьи не слышал голоса,
Сияли силою надзвездной
Всевидящие небеса.

Вот я добрался до границы.
Проснулись клены вдалеке
И разговаривали птицы
На незнакомом языке.

Под ними день новорожденный,
Я к ним прислушался: скворцы,
Но понял вдруг, что эти клены,
А я, и птицы - мертвецы.

И то, что зарубежным краем
Казалось на пути моем,
Лишь вымысел. И вряд ли знаем:
Мы умерли или живем?

(1999)

Path

I walked alone, unheard
along a strange star-lit path.

Then I reached a border
where maples rose far ahead
and starlings chattered
in a foreign language.

I listened to the birds
and watched the maples
but as morning came
I saw we were all corpses.

In that morning,
the strange star-lit road
began to seem unreal
and life and death unknowable.

[OS and YG]

Гнездо

Дуб стоит, как прежде, одинокий,
Только небо веселей и чище,
С прутиками в клювах две сороки
Строить начали свое жилище.

В сущности, я тоже одинокий,
Но скорей не дерево, а птица,
Как гнездо, я строю эти строки.
Чтоб весне нашлось, где поселиться.

(1999)

Nest

A lone oak
clear bright sky
magpies, twigs in beaks
nest-build.

I'm as lonely as the oak
but like a bird
I build these lines
into a home for the spring.

[OS and YG]

Надпись На Восточной Книге

Зачем непрочные страницы множить
И в упоенье, в темноте надменной
Выделывать сомнительный товар?

Приходит время, как халиф Омар,
Чтоб ненароком книги уничтожить
За исключением одной - священной.

(1983)

Handwriting on the Eastern Book

Why write words on a page
in a trance of inspiration
and make something so approximate

so readily supervened
as when Kalif Omar
destroyed all but the Holy Book.

[SP and YG]

Умер мой одногодок.

Охватила тоска,
Для словесных находок
Не ищу я листка.

Может, встретимся скоро,
Хорошо б не в аду,
Где врата без затвора:
Но войду - не уйду.

Длились годы особо,
Каждый с грузом вины,
Мы по-разному оба
Перед Богом грешны.

Он не верил, я верил,
Он блистал, я мерцал,
Рок беззлобно похерил
Наших буквиц навал.

А кругом так безлюдно,
А мой путь так нелеп,
Так мне дышится трудно,
Так мне горек мой хлеб.

(1998)

Dead Friend of My Own Age

I'm in anguish –
depressed, wordless,
paper unlooked for.

Maybe we'll meet soon
and it'll be better than this hell
where the gates have no bolts
but I'm still here, and won't leave.

The years have drawn out,
each with the weight of our guilt.
We were different before God
in our guilt.

He was an atheist, I a believer.
He beamed, I sparkled.
Heaps of letters crossed
between us by kind fate.

My surroundings are uninhabited
my journey is mindless
my breath is stifled
my bread is the bread of affliction

[OS and YG]

Моисей Говорит О Торе

Она существовала до меня.
Ее слова из черного огня

На белом обозначены огне
И сказаны они сегодня мне,

Слова, услышанные мной с небес,
На камне начертал я, резьборез.

Нет в мире камня крепче и прочней,
Никто ему не равен из камней.

Вас ждут богатства, но и глад, и мор,
И власть, и рабство, слава и позор,

Вас убивая, примут племена
Заветы ваши, ваши имена.

Вам будут редко воздавать хвалу,
Вас будут вешать, превращать в золу,

Но мук сильнее всех и всех словес
Слова, ниспосланные вам с небес.

Как жизнь и смерть весом их вечный вес,
Их начертал на камне резьборез.

(1998)

Moses Speaks About Torah

Its words existed before I did,
words made from black fire,

words written on the whitest fire,
and they were told to me today.

I, who heard the words from heaven,
was the mason who carved them in stone.

No stone in the world was as strong and hard,
no other can equal it.

Riches await you but also hunger, plague,
power, slavery, glory, disgrace.

Death will be the legacy of your tribes,
generations and namesakes.

Rarely will you be praised or be paid homage,
you will wear the noose and return to ash.

These are the words sent down to us from heaven,
like life and death they weigh eternal,
they were carved in stone by a mason.

[OS and YG]

Вольный перевод

Над крышей блещет небосклон.
Густою кроной
Шумит над этой крышей клен
Темно-зеленый.

Как нежен колокольный звон!
Он вверх стремится,
Ему, слетевшая на клен,
Внимает птица,

О, Господи, как жизнь проста!
День снова прожит
И городская маета
Нас не тревожит,

Но плачу я на склоне дней,
Живу, седею, —
Что стало с юностью моей?

(1999)

Verlaine

Above its roof
the thick dark canopy
of a maple rustles
then heaven's vault shines.

How gently the toll of its bell
reaches the Almighty
carried by the maple
heard by a bird.

My God
we live simply now,
each day's quiet
far from the city.

I am going grey
my days are numbered.
Where's my youth,
What have I done to it?

(After 'Wisdom')

[OS and YG]

Еще и плотью не оделись души,

И прах - травой, и небо - синевой,
Еще вода не отошла от суши,
И свет был слеп во тьме довековой,
Еще неизреченным было слово,
И мысль спала в тиши предгрозовой,
И смерть не знала теплоты живого,
А я уже тебя любил.
И боль моя свою постигла смелость,
И свет прозрел во тьме, и твердь земли,
От влаги отделясь, травой оделась,
И души плоть впервые обрели,
И мысль проснулась в мирозданье новом,
И время, уходящее вдали,
Увидела она и стала словом
И мерою всего, что есть.

(1972)

Souls Naked of Flesh

Dust without grass
skies without blue
water and land undivided
light, yet blind in darkness.

The word was unutterable,
the other was asleep in the silence before the storm,
life's warmth was unknown to death
but I already loved you.

Pain has understood my courage
light has learned to see
hard earth cut from the water
is dressed in grass,

souls now wear flesh
thought has woken up, seen,
become the word, the measure of all existing things
and time passes by in the distance.

[MP and YG]

Договор

Если в воздухе пахло землею
Или рвался снаряд в вышине,
Договор между Богом и мною
Открывался мне в дымном огне.

И я шел нескончаемым адом,
Телом раб, но душой господин,
И хотя были тысячи рядом,
Я всегда оставался один.

(1948)

The Covenant

After a mine blasted
the smell of earth into the air

the covenant between us, God,
opened inside me,

in smoke, in fire
an endless inferno enslaved my body

endless solitude exiled my soul
though thousands of people were nearby.

[YG]

Дорога

Лежит в кювете грязный цыганенок,
А рядом с ним, косясь на свет машин,

Стоит курчавый, вежливый ягненок
И женственный, как молодой раввин.

Горячий, ясный вечер, и дорога,
И все цветы лесные с их пыльцой,

И ты внезапно открываешь Бога
В своем родстве с цыганом и овцой.

(1961)

Road

In a roadside ditch
on a hot evening
thick with pollen
a gypsy boy lies next to a lamb

who glances past the wild flowers
at the traffic, innocent as a young rabbi

and suddenly you discover God
in the way you see them.

[SM and YG]

"В Неверии, Неволе, Нелюбви"

В неверии, неволе, нелюбви,
В беседах о войне, дороговизне,
Как сладко лгать себе, что дни твои -
Еще не жизнь, а ожиданье жизни.

Кто скажет, как наступит новый день?
По-человечьи запоет ли птица,
Иль молнией расколотая тень
Раздастся и грозою разразится?

Но той грозы жестоким голосам
Ты весело, всем сердцем отзовешься,
Ушам не веря и не зная сам,
Чему ты рад и почему смеешься

(1940)

Ye of Little Faith

speak about the cost of war
the sweet illusion that life's not begun,
of how you are yet to be born.

Who can say what day will bring?
Will birds speak? Will lightning cleave shadows
in thunder storms, and make you welcome explosions?

Would you trust yourself,
would you ask why you're laughing?

(After 'In no faith, no freedom, no love'.)

[YG]

Счастье

Хорошо мне торчать в номерах бобылем,
    По казачьим станицам бродить,
Называть молодое вино чихирем,
    Равнодушно торговок бранить.

Ах, у скряги земли столько спрятано мест,
    Но к сокровищам ключ я нашел.
Это просто совсем: если жить надоест, –
    Взял под мышку портфель - и пошел.

Из аула в аул я шатаюсь, но так
    Забывают дорогу назад.
Там арабскими кличками кличут собак,
    Над могилами жерди стоят.

Это знак, что великий смельчак погребен,
    Мне ж, по правде сказать, наплевать,
Лишь бы воздух был чист, и глубок небосклон,
    И вокруг ни души не видать.

Вот уже за спиною мечеть и погост,
    И долина блестит вдалеке.
Полумесяцем там перекинулся мост,
    В безымянной колеблясь реке.

Очевидно, река здесь недавно бежит,
    Изменила недавно русло.
Там, где раньше бежала, там щебень лежит,
    И каменья чисты, как стекло.

Долго странствовать буду. Когда же назад
    Я вернусь, не увижу реки:
Только россыпи щебня на солнце блестят,
    Только иверни да кругляки!

Оскверню ли я землю хулой иль хвалой?
    Постою, погляжу и пойду.
За скалой многоуглой, за каменной мглой
    Безымянной рекой пропаду.

(1938)

Bliss

I'm a bachelor who loves to stay in hotels,
visit Cossack stanitsas, order chirchir,
curse with market women, then move on
to unlock the miserly earth's secrets

you forget the way home in the fresh air, deep sky
of places that use Arabic nicknames,
and mark a hero's tomb with a tapered shaft.
Look, I've already passed the mosque, the graveyard

a valley shines in the distance straddled by a bridge
as white as a crescent moon in a nameless river
which shifts a bed of glassy rubble as it meanders.
By the time I get back here the river will be dry

leaving sticks, logs, a bed of shale in the sun
will I bless or curse the parched earth? I'll stop a while
then walk away in the stony haze, past jagged rocks
until I disappear, a nameless river

[SM and YG]

У полустанка

Дуб, от множества годов сутулый,
Слушать с упоением готов
Самолетов эллинские гулы,
Русские глаголы поездов.

Утро хорошо на полустанке,
А весной особенно светло
Небо голубое, как с изнанки
Голубя вспорхнувшего крыло.

Ночью столько шорохов и звонов,
Быстро вспыхивают светляки,
Окна убегающих вагонов,
Звездочек живые угольки.

Не стареть бы, не слабеть, не сохнуть,
А дышать, и думать, и смотреть,
Вдруг от грома вешнего оглохнуть,
С молнией сгореть.

(1969)

In Limbo

A gnarled oak stoops
ready to listen
to the Hellenic drone of planes
to the Russian lexicon of rail-cars.

Morning's always good,
Spring light's best
the sky's blue, blue as the flash
under a pigeon's wing.

Night rustles, jangles,
fire-flies flash
car windows streak
stars glower.

Don't age, tire, lose sap,
breathe, think, look, be deafened
by the clap of forest thunder
or burned by lightning

[SM and YG]

Что Говорит Родник

С опаской сходим с высоты,
Так близко облака над нами
Там, где беседует с камнями
Родник небесной чистоты.

Губительны крутые глыбы,
Насторожился проводник...
О, если мы узнать могли бы,
Что говорит камням родник!

Он движется движеньем робким.
Не всем слышны слова его.
Лишь незаметным внятно тропкам
Его небесное родство.

(1997)

The Descent

We climb down through rivers
with clouds behind us
as the spring of life
talks to the silt

tries to reason with scree
and our guide thinks, *if only
we could understand* . . .

but only the rushing water
hears the word, carries the whisper
in its current

[YG]

Был царствия войны тяжелый год.

В тот год весна к нам дважды приходила,
А в третий раз она пришла в обход,

Затем, что всюду стражу находила
Безжалостной зимы. Был долог путь,
И, поднимаясь медленно, светила

Дрожали в сером небе, точно ртуть.
Тельца и Близнецов мерцали знаки,
Но в свете дня была густая муть,

Как бы в глазах взбесившейся собаки.
Три раза реки прятались во льду.
Три раза полдни прятались во мраке.

(1947)

Neither War nor its Sentries Relented

They sealed us in 'til May that year
Spring failed twice and used a detour
to get to us a third time.

The moon rose slowly
shivered in the grey nights
Taurus and Gemini flickered like beads of mercury.

The days were thick with mist
like the blurred eyes of rabid dogs.

Three times the rivers hid under the ice
the moon in darkness.

[YG]

Зимний Закат

Вот я вижу тебя сквозь очередь,
Где в былое пятятся годы,
Соименница дерзкой дочери
Сандомирского воеводы.

Как привыкла ты, пообедали
В метростроевской мы обжорке,
На закате зимнем проведали
Те, что помнила ты, задворки.

Вот любуемся мы домишками
И церквами Замоскворечья.
На тебе, как на князе Мышкине,
Тонкий плащ топорщил оплечья.

О декабрьской забыв суровости,
Мне своим говорком московским
Сообщила старые новости
О Бальмонте, о Мережковском.

Притворились, что не заметили,
Как над нами кружится стужа.
Где присяжные? Где свидетели?
Где Париж? Где погибель мужа?

А порой от намека слабого
Поднималась надменно бровка...
Далека, далека Елабуга
И татарская та веревка.

(1984)

Winter Sunset at the Diner
addressed to Marina Tsvetaeva

Where's Paris now
or the Soviet judge and jury
the witnesses?
Sandomirsky's brave daughter,
through the queues of railway builders
jostling for lunch it's only you
I can still see.

We left at sunset
walked the alleys, yards, churches
behind the Moskva,
ignored cold December –
your thin mackintosh
was as skewed as Myshkin's cloak
as you gave me old news
of Merezhkovsky and Balmont,
nineteen to the dozen
in your Muscovite accent.

We ignored the frost,
you raised your eyebrows
to silence questions.
Elabuga and that Tartar rope
were a long way away.

[YG]

Похороны

Умерла Татьяна Васильевна,
Наша маленькая, близорукая,
Обескровлена, обессилена
Восемнадцатилетнею мукою.

С ней прощаются нежно и просто,
Без молитвы и суеты,
Шаповалов из Княж-Погоста,
Яков Горовиц из Ухты.

Для чего копаться в истории,
Как возникли навет и поклеп?
Но когда опускался гроб
В государственном крематории, -

Побелевшая от обид,
Горем каторжным изнуренная,
Покоренная, примиренная,
Зарыдала тундра навзрыд.

Это раны раскрылись живые,
Это крови хлестала струя,
Это плакало сердце России -
Пятьдесят восьмая статья.

И пока нам, грешным, не терпится
Изменить иль обдумать судьбу,
Наша маленькая страстотерпица
Входит в пламя - уже в гробу.

Но к чему о скорби всеобщей
Говорить с усмешкою злой?
Но к чему говорить об усопшей,
Что святая стала золой?

Помянуть бы ее, как водится
От языческих лет славянства...
Но друзья постепенно расходятся,
Их Москвы поглощает пространство.

Лишь безмолвно стоят у моста,
Посреди городской духоты,
Шаповалов из Княж-Погоста,
Яков Горовиц из Ухты.

(1958)

Funeral

Emaciated by her eighteen year term,
our tiny, myopic Tatyana Vasilievna's died.
Shapovalov and Horowitz from the gulag
say a simple goodbye, no prayers, no ritual;
why search for the betrayer as the coffin slides
into the City's crematorium?

The exhausted tundra, whitened by insults,
beaten by hard labour, sobs, bleeds from old wounds,
cries out from Russia's heart –
dissident.

Why are we sinners so keen
to ruminate over destiny
while our tiny surrogate meets it –
why do we call her a saint
instead of remembering her
like pagans with Slavic rites?

Her friends are going now
to be swallowed up in Moscow's spaces,
only Shapovalov and Horowitz
remain in the airless City.

[YG]

Молчащие

Ты прав, конечно. Чем печаль печальней,
Тем молчаливей. Потому-то лес
Нам кажется большой исповедальней,
Чуждающейся выспренних словес.

Есть у деревьев, лиственных и хвойных,
Бесчисленные способы страдать
И нет ни одного, чтоб передать
Свое отчаянье... Мы, в наших войнах

И днях затишья, умножаем чад
Речей, ругательств, жалоб и смятений,
Живя среди чувствительных растений,
Кричим и плачем... А они молчат.

(1963)

The Silent

You're right of course,
the deeper the sadness
the quieter it is.
That's why the forest
seems like a big confessional,
a place to whisper.

The pine, the oak
have endless ways to suffer
but not one to describe suffering.

We in our wars and peace
multiply the fumes of speech;
complaints, confusion, curses
live among the sensitive plants,
we howl and scream and swear
and they keep silent.

[YG]

Ереванская Роза

Ереванская роза
Мерным слогом воркует,
Гармонически плачет навзрыд.
Ереванская проза
Мастерит, и торгует,
И кричит, некрасиво кричит.
Ереванскую розу -
Вздох и целую фразу -
Понимаешь: настолько проста.
Ереванскую прозу
Понимаешь не сразу,
Потому, что во всем разлита -
В старике, прищемившем
Левантийские четки
Там, где брызги фонтана летят,
В малыше, устремившем
Свой пытливый и кроткий,
Умудренный страданием взгляд.
Будто знался он с теми,
Чья душа негасима,
Кто в далеком исчез далеке,
Будто где-то в эдеме
Он встречал серафима
С ереванской розой в руке.

(1965)

The Rose of Yerevan

coos in cadenced phrases,
cries in uncontrolled harmonics.
The prose of Yerevan
touts and tempts
cajoles and pleads.
The rose of Yerevan
sighs a whole sentence
you can understand.
The prose of Yerevan
takes longer to know
it's spilt around or measured
like an old man counting prayer beads.
The prose of Yerevan
is like the splash of a fountain's play,
the fix of an infant's gaze
mild and wise with suffering
as though he's known the subsisting souls
of bodies disappeared in time,
as though he'd met a seraph who held a rose of Yerevan
in his hand.

[YG]

Молодая Мать

Лежала Настенька на печке,
Начфин проезжий - на полу.
Посапывали две овечки
За рукомойником в углу.
В окне белела смутно вишня,
В кустах таился частокол.
И старой бабке стало слышно,
Как босиком начфин прошел.
Ее испуг, его досада
И тихий жаркий разговор.
– Не надо, дяденька, не надо!
– Нет, надо! - отвечал майор.
Не на Дону, уже за Бугом
Начфин ведет свои дела,
Но не отделалась испугом,
Мальчонку Настя родила.
Черты бессмысленного счастья,
Любви бессмысленной черты, -
Пленяет и пугает Настя
Сияньем юной красоты.
Каким-то робким просветленьем,
Понятным только ей одной,
Слегка лукавым удивленьем
Пред сладкой радостью земной.
Она совсем еще невинна
И целомудренна, как мать.
Еще не могут глазки сына
Ей никого напоминать.
Кого же? Вишню с белой пеной?
Овечек? Частокол в кустах?
Каков собою был военный:
Красив ли? Молод ли? В годах?
Все горечи еще далёки,
Еще таит седая рань
Станичниц грубые попреки,
И утешения, и брань.
Она сойдет с ребенком к Дону,
Когда в цветах забродит хмель,
Когда Сикстинскую мадонну
С нее напишет Рафаэль.

(1955)

The Cossack Mother

Nastenka's on her hearth
an intruder's on her floor
lambs wheeze behind the wash bowl
a cherry tree blanches the window
a sturdy fence hides in the bushes.

An old Cossack woman heard
the officer creep in uninvited
heard his rage, her fear, *don't, don't,*
heard him hurt her.

But that isn't the end
Nastenka has a son, earth's surprise.
She understands nothing,
his eyes remind her of no one,
who then will she see in them?
Cherry blossom, lambs, a sturdy fence?
What did the officer look like?
Was he young, old? The pain's forgotten.
Grey haired dawn hides the judgment of the Bug River,
the comfort, the abuse.
When the hop flowers fade
she'll take her son to the village of Don
and Raphael will see her and use her as his model
for the Sistine Madonna.

[YG]

В Калмыцкой Степи

Днем

В долине плоской, как доска,
Чернеют овцы и собаки –
Начертанные кем-то знаки
Неведомого языка.
Песок и солнце жгут их колко,
А я пытаюсь их прочесть,
Забыв про шифер и про жесть
Степного пыльного поселка.
Вдруг клинописному письму
И я сумею научиться,
Но смысл, который в нем таится,
Я не открою никому.

Ночью

О степь калмыцкая с двоякой
Субстанцией ночной,
Когда братаются два мрака:
Воздушный и степной.
Здесь образ неба так нагляден,
Как будто степь видна,
В нем столько же бугров и впадин,
Как у степного дна.
Здесь понял я, что мир загробный
Земным стезям сродни,
Здесь звездам - редкие - подобны
Степных жилищ огни.
Здесь видел я, как вспыхнул разум
Небесной чистоты
В том желтоскулом, узкоглазом,
Который гнал гурты.

(1984)

The Kalmyk Steppe

In The Daytime

Someone marks a flat vale with black sheep and dogs
burned and bitten by the sun and sand.
They create a language I try to read.

I've forgotten about the slate and tin
of a dusty settlement in the steppe.
What if I could learn this wedge writing?
But its meaning is hidden, unknowable.

At Night

On the Kalmyk steppe
painted double with night
two types of dark become brothers,
the sky, the earth.

The skies are as humped and hollowed as the steppe,
as solid as this expanse of ground.

It was here I understood that this world and the next
are just the same, that Kalmyk windows shine like stars.

It was here I saw heaven's purity and reason, driving herds,
he had narrow eyes and yellow cheek bones.

[YG]

На Тянь-Шане

Бьется бабочка в горле кумгана,
Спит на жердочке беркут седой,
И глядит них Зигмунд Сметана,
Элегантный варшавский портной.
Издалёка занес его случай,
А другие исчезли в золе,
Там, за проволокою колючей,
И теперь он один на земле.
В мастерскую, кружась над саманом,
Залетает листок невзначай.
Над горами — туман. За туманом —
Вы подумайте только — Китай!
В этот час появляются люди:
Коновод на кобылке Сафо,
И семейство верхом верблюде,
И в вельветовой куртке райфо.
День в пыли исчезает как всадник,
Овцы тихо вбегают в закут.
Зябко прячет листы виноградник,
И опресноки в юрте пекут.
Точно так их пекли в Галилее,
Под навесом, вечерней порой...
И стоит с сантиметром на шее
Элегантный варшавский портной.
Не соринка в глазу, не слезинка —
Это жжет его мертвым огнем,
Это ставшая прахом Треблинка
Жгучий пепел оставила в нем.

(1948)

In the Tian Shan

A dapper Warsaw tailor watches
a butterfly knock against the throat of a kumgan.
A grey haired golden eagle sleeps on a perch.

Others became ash behind barbed wire
but Zigismund Smetana ends up here,
alone on earth, a single leaf swirls
around his hut.

The mountains are foggy.
Behind them, just think, there's China.

People begin to arrive now,
Sappho with the leader in her saddle,
RAYFO's tax man in corduroy,
a camel and a family

Daylight disappears in dust like a horseman,
quiet sheep flock to their pens,
frozen vineyards hide their leaves,

ovens bake matzas inside the yurts
just as they did in Galilee.

The tailor stands pristine, spotless
under an awning at dusk,
his tape measure round his neck.

He's charred by dead fire.
Treblinka became dust
and left burning embers inside him.

[YG]

Размышления В Сараеве

Мечеть в Сараеве, где стрелки на часах
Магометанское показывают время,
Где птицы тюркские - в славянских голосах,
       Где Бог обозначает племя,
Где ангелы грустят на разных небесах.

Улыбка юная монаха-босняка
И феска плоская печального сефарда.
    Народы сдвинулись, как скалы и века,
       И серафимский запах нарда
Волна Авзонии несет издалека.

Одежда, говоры, базары и дворы
 Здесь дышат нацией, повсюду вавилоны,
 Столпотворения последние костры.
       Иль не един разноплеменный
Сей мир, и все его двуногие миры?

На узкой улице прочел я след ноги
 Увековеченный, - и понял страшный принцип
 Столетья нашего, я услыхал шаги
       И выстрел твой, Гаврила Принцип,
Дошедшие до нас, до тундры и тайги.

 Когда в эрцгерцога ты выстрел произвел,
Чернорубашечный поход на Рим насытил
Ты кровью собственной, раскол марксистских школ
       Ты возвестил, ты предвосхитил
Рев мюнхенских пивных и сталинский глагол.

Тогда-то ожили понятие вождей,
Камлание жреца - предвиденья замена,
Я здесь в Сараеве, почувствовал больней,
       Что мы вернулись в род, в колено,
Сменили стойбищем сообщество людей..

Всегда пугает ночь, особенно в чужом,
В нерусском городе. Какая в ней тревога!
Вот милицейские машины за углом,
   Их много, даже слишком много,
И крики близятся, как равномерный гром.

Студенты-бунтари нестройный режут круг
Толпы на площади, но почему-то снова
К ней возвращаются. Не силу, а недуг
   Мятежное рождает слово,
И одиноко мне, и горько стало вдруг.

(1968)

Reflections in Sarajevo

The mosque in Sarajevo
where the clock hands show Muslim time,
Turkish birds sing Slavic songs.

God calls a tribe a place
where angels are unhappy
in different heavens,

the youthful smile of a Bosnian monk,
the sad face of a Sephardi in his tarbush,

the seraph smell of spikenard from distant Avsonia
cloth, dialects, markets, yards, breathe with a nation.

Everywhere there are Babylons, the last fires of Babel,
isn't this a two legged world of tribes united in their
differences?

In a narrow street I read a footstep commemorated
and realize the terrible principle of our century.

I heard your footsteps, your bullet, Gavrilo Princip,
when you shot at Archduke Franz Ferdinand
it reached the tundra and the taiga,

your blood fuelled the crusade of the Black Shirts in Rome,
named the Marxist split, held back Stalin's word,
and the roar of Munich's beer houses

brought the notion of leaders to life,
a shamanistic ritual of a priest,
a replacement of a vision.

In Sarajevo I suffered,
felt how we became racial, tribal,
sacrificed community.

Night always scares me,
especially in a town away from Russia.
There were so many police cars, round every corner.

Shouting closed in like steady thunder,
the student protest cut in and out
of the uneven crowd in the square.

They were diseased not empowered
by their rebellion and suddenly
I felt lonely and bitter.

[YG]

Когда в слова я буквы складыва

Когда в слова я буквы складывал
И смыслу помогал родиться,
Уже я смутно предугадывал,
Как мной судьба распорядится,

Как я не дорасту до форточки,
А тело мне сожмут поводья,
Как сохраню до смерти черточки
Пугливого простонародья.

Век сумасшедший мне сопутствовал,
Подняв свирепое дреколье,
И в детстве я уже предчувствовал
Свое мятежное безволье.

Но жизнь моя была таинственна,
И жил я, странно понимая,
Что в мире существует истина
Зиждительная, неземная,

И если приходил в отчаянье
От всепобедного развала,
Я радость находил в раскаянье,
И силу слабость мне давала.

(1976)

When I was Putting Letters Together into Words

and helping their meaning along,
I had a sense of how my life would go,
I wouldn't ever grow tall enough
to close window vents, I'd champ at the bit,
die with the face of an ordinary, frightened man,
the crazy age would raise its batons
against my rebellious passivity.

But my life was mysterious, with a strange understanding
of metaphysical truth in the creative world,
and if I despaired, from the all-victorious breakdown,
I found joy in repentance and my weakness gave me
strength.

[YG]

У Моря

Шумели волны под огнем маячным,
Я слушал их, и мне морской прибой
Казался однозвучным, однозначным:
Я молод был, я полон был собой.
Но вот теперь, иною сутью полный,
Опять стою у моря, и опять
Со мною разговаривают волны,
И я их начинаю понимать.
Есть волны-иволги и волны-прачки,
Есть волны-злыдни, волны-колдуны.
Заклятьями сменяются заплачки
И бранью - стон из гулкой глубины.
Есть волны белые и полукровки,
Чья робость вдруг становится дерзка,
Есть волны - круглобедрые торговки,
Торгующие кипенью с лотка.
Одни трепещут бегло и воздушно,
Другие - тугодумные умы...
Природа не бывает равнодушна,
Всегда ей нужно стать такой, как мы.
Природа - переводческая калька:
Мы подлинник, а копия она.
В былые дни была иною галька
И по-иному думала волна.

(1965)

By the Sea

The waves crashed under the flicker of the lighthouse
and I, in my ignorance, heard a monotone.
Years later the sea speaks to me and I begin to understand
there are birds and laundresses, sprites and sorcerers
laments and curses, moans and profanity, white horses
and half breeds who rear up unexpectedly.
There are waves who are salesgirls with buxom hips
who sell foam from the counter, they tremble fluent or airy.
Nature can't be indifferent, she always mimics us
like a loan, a translation; we're the blueprint she's the copy.
Once upon a time the pebble was different
and so the wave was different.

[YG]

Appendix

Translation from Lipkin's Journals by Robert and Elizabeth Chandler

Lipkin as a Memoirist

A s well as being a poet and translator of poetry, Semyon Lipkin also wrote several hundred pages of memoirs. Many of these are about other poets, including Akhmatova, Tsvetaeva and Zabolotsky. The longest chapter – which I hope will one day be translated in full – is devoted to Vasily Grossman, who was a friend of Lipkin's. Some of the most interesting passages are about the friendship between Vasily Grossman and Andrey Platonov, the two greatest Russian prose-writers of the last century. I am grateful to Yvonne Green for making space, in this volume, for a brief extract:

When something was read aloud to him, Platonov did not often voice his opinion. Instead, he would repeat several times some phrase that he especially liked, and, on his lips, the phrase would take on a particular meaning. When he repeated a line from my poem 'To Hide one's Tracks', I understood that his own experience of life had endowed this line with some particular significance for him. When Grossman read us chapters from his novel For a Just Cause, it was the same; Platonov did not say anything – he simply repeated phrases that had made a particular impression on him.

Platonov read two of his own works aloud in my presence: his wonderful novella Dzhan, in which, with biblical simplicity and vividness, he tells the story of a small nomadic tribe (their name, the Dzhan, is a Persian word meaning 'soul')[1] wandering about the deserts of Central Asis in the 1930s; and a short story about a soldier who returns home to a wife who betrayed him while he was away fighting. When he read his own work, Platonov was always the first to laugh when he came to a funny passage.

I do not remember Platonov making long pronouncements about anything. Often he hemmed and hawed, or muttered under his breath, his lips pursed. And this muttering and pursing of the lips would seem to me more intelligent and meaningful than many people's words. But

---

[1] The English version, published by Harvill Secker in the U.K. and NYRB Classics in the USA, is titled *Soul*.

Platonov was able to get to the crux of a matter and find concise and vivid words for what mattered most.

I only once remember Platonov speaking at length about literary matters. He said that not every servile word wins the favour of the authorities; it is essential that the servile word be said at the right time. It achieves nothing if it is pronounced too late, and it often enrages the authorities if it is said too early – the authorities hate people who run too far ahead of them.

I remember one other trait of Platonov's: no item of literary or political news, no matter how absurd or astounding, could ever surprise him. He would always reply in the same calm tone, and with the same words: *A free thing!* [In Russian: *Svobodnaya veshch!* The implication of this little-known idiom, pronounced with at least a metaphorical shrug of the shoulders, is that things and events are free to go their own way – that 'Anything can happen!'. The Russian-American scholar Olga Meerson has used this favourite phrase of Platonov's as the title of an important book about him.]

They loved each other – Grossman, who, during the war years was an honoured figure and a member of the Board of the Writers' Union, and the persecuted Platonov, whose name meant nothing to most readers. Both Grossman and Platonov hated servile literature. Even in regard to writers generally seen as decent figures, even in regard to their own friends, they were intolerant of half-truths, posing, empty verbiage and affectations.

But Grossman, both in his own writings and in his general tastes – whether we are talking about literature, art or music – was more loyal to tradition, to the Russian and West European classics of the nineteenth and early twentieth centuries – while Platonov was more independent in his judgments. Both were drawn to simple people, to workers and peasants, but, in Grossman's case, this sprang from the social-democrat views of his youth, which he had perhaps imbibed from his father Semyon Osipovich, who had once been a Menshevik, whereas in Platonov's case this was a part of the reverence he felt for life in all its simplest manifestations of life, both in nature and human society.

I remember the exultation with which Platonov spoke of his days as an engine driver: 'The engine is in good working order, and you are flying, the earth and sky are coming towards you, and you are master of the whole space of the world.' Neither Platonov nor Grossman believed in God, but they did not – like many of my contemporaries – laugh at my own religious beliefs. I would say that they both held to a materialist philosophy, but Grossman, at least for many years, saw himself as a Marxist, whereas Platonov's materialism was a pantheistic materialism, close to the world-view of Fyodorov.

Once I recounted to both of them an episode from the Mahabharata. Some pilgrims, nearing the goal of their pilgrimage, see some cowpats on the path and – afraid lest even glancing at such impurity will pollute their pious intent – hurry to wash their bodies in the river. But just then the God Indra arises from the cowpats and says, 'Pitiful people – it was I who had transformed myself into those cowpats, for there is nothing on Earth that is either pure or impure.'

Grossman said, 'Interesting.' But Platonov slowly repeated, 'For there is nothing on Earth that is either pure or impure.'

After the War was over, the three of us sometimes used to sit together on the Tverskoy Boulevard, on a bench opposite the windows of Platonov's apartment. One of our favourite activities was composing stories about some passer-by or other who had attracted our attention. My own efforts were pallid, and it is not myself I want to talk about, but both Grossman and Platonov revealed much of themselves in this light-hearted game. Grossman's stories were full of detail. If he thought that the passer-by was an accountant, then he would add that the man worked in a factory that made sweets. If he thought that the passer-by was a worker, he would add that he worked in an electrical factory. This would be followed by portraits of the man's wife and children and his old drunkard of a father, who was from the town of Mozhaisk. Platonov's stories were very different. They had little in the way of plot, and what was portrayed in them was the person's inner life, which was both unusual and simple, like the life of a plant.

I also remember another occasion, at the height of the 'Struggle against Cosmopolitanism' [a euphemism widely used during Stalin's antisemitic campaign of 1948–1953 – R.C.], when the three of us were sitting on this same bench. Grossman went off to get cigarettes from the kiosk on the corner, and just then Ivan Nikanorovich Rozanov – a very sweet old man, a professor with a great love of poetry – shuffled up to us and said, showing his few long teeth in a broad smile, 'You can feel how the air's become cleaner. There's no longer such a stink of garlic.' And off he went on his way, leaning on his stick. Old age had evidently led him to forget about my own Jewish origin. When Grossman came back with his cigarettes, I told him what had happened. Taken aback for a moment, Grossman just said, 'What an eccentric old man!' Then he laid into me and Platonov, shouting and swearing: why hadn't we answered these vile words? Why had we just listened submissively? Platonov said feebly, 'All right, all right, Vasya,' but he was embarrassed. In *Life and Fate* Grossman has an old teacher come out with these same words about the stink of garlic.

When Platonov fell ill, Grossman visited him almost every day. Platonov had caught tuberculosis from his dying son – in some kind of mad fit he had kissed him on the lips.[2] Once Grossman and I visited Platonov together. I shall never forget the sharp brilliance of the long anguish in Platonov's sunken eyes, his thin yellow face, his constant quiet coughing.

Grossman was shaken by Platonov's death. And, as he wrote to me from his dacha not long afterwards, he was 'exhausted from all the organizational tasks linked to the funeral, that no one else in the Writers' Union had wanted to be bothered with.'

I remember the moving speech that Grossman gave over his friend's coffin in the presence of the few people who had come to the Writers' Union to remember Platonov. This speech was an intelligent and deeply pained tribute to a writer who died without proper recognition, almost unknown. It was a long time before it became possible to publish this speech. In January 1960, however, Grossman wrote to me, 'I've been invited to speak about Andrey Platonov on the radio. I've agreed; I've written a short article. We'll see whether or not anything comes of this. Maybe I'll have more luck in this genre – as an akyn [a Kirghiz folk-poet – R.C.] singing laments.

Grossman did indeed read on the radio his article based on what he had said at Platonov's funeral. It was the first sensible and worthwhile word said in Russia about Platonov. The article was later published in the journal Literary Russia as a review of one of the first posthumous collections of Platonov's work. Few people knew of Platonov when Grossman described him there as 'a writer who wanted to understand the most complicated – which really means the most simple – foundations of human existence.'

---

[2] Platonov's son Platon had been sent to a labour camp in 1938, at the age of fifteen. He was released in 1940, but by then he had tuberculosis, and he died in 1943. It is impossible to be sure whether Lipkin's story about Platonov kissing his son on the lips is true, or whether it is just one of the many myths that have grown up around Platonov.

Right up until the end of his life Grossman continued to reminisce about Platonov and to re-read him. In one of his last letters to me, he wrote, 'I'm reading Platonov's stories. There is great power in these stories – 'Takyr', 'The Third Son', 'Fro'. It is as if you are in the desert and you hear the voice of a friend – this brings both joy and pain.'

Semyon Lipkin, Kvadriga (Moscow: Agraf, 1997), pp. 523-528 (abridged)

Translation © by Robert & Elizabeth Chandler, March 2011

Extract from Robert Chandler's Introduction to Vasily Grossman's *The Road* (2010 Maclehose Press) in which Robert Chandler details the part Lipkin played in preserving Grossman's *Life and Fate* for publication

The other sorrow that hung over Grossman's last years was the 'arrest' – as Russians still refer to it – of *Life and Fate*. In October 1960, against the advice of both Lipkin and Zabolotskaya, Grossman delivered the manuscript to the editors of *Znamya*. It was the height of Khrushchev's 'Thaw' and Grossman seems to have believed that *Life and Fate* could be published, even though one of its central themes is the identity of Nazism and Stalinism. Grossman is generally thought to have behaved naively, but he was evidently clear-headed enough to take precautions. He himself censored about fifteen per cent of the text he submitted.[1] He left a copy of the complete typescript with Lipkin, and he entrusted his original manuscript to Lyolya Klestova,[2] a friend from his student days who had no connection with the literary world.

In February 1961, three KGB officers came to Grossman's apartment. They confiscated the typescript and everything bearing any relation to it, even carbon paper and typing ribbons. This is one of only two occasions when the Soviet authorities 'arrested' a book while leaving the writer at liberty; no other book, apart from *The Gulag Archipelago*, was ever considered so dangerous.[3] Grossman refused to sign an undertaking not to speak of this visit. He agreed to take the KGB officers to his two typists and to his cousin Viktor Sherentsis in order for them to confiscate other copies of the typescript, but he may well have done this in the hope of deflecting attention from the copies he had left with Lipkin and Klestova.[4] The KGB, in any case, did not find the remaining copies, even though they evidently made considerable efforts. According to Tatiana Menaker, a distant younger relative of Grossman's, they went to Viktor Sherentsis's dacha and dug up the whole of his vegetable garden.[5]

In 1975, more than ten years after Grossman's death, Lipkin asked the writer Vladimir Voinovich to help get *Life and Fate* published in the West. After making what turned out to be an inadequate microfilm, Voinovich asked Andrey Sakharov to make a second microfilm; Voinovich then sent this abroad. The microfilm reached Vladimir Maksimov, the chief editor of the émigré journal *Kontinent*, but

Maksimov published only a few somewhat randomly chosen chapters; his lack of interest probably stemmed from his antisemitism. In 1977 Voinovich made a third microfilm, which he entrusted – together with his first, poor-quality microfilm – to an Austrian professor, Rosemarie Ziegler. These two microfilms reached Yefim Etkind, a writer and scholar then living in Paris. With the help of a colleague, Shimon Markish, Etkind established an almost complete text; this was not easy, since both microfilms were flawed. Several émigré publishing houses then turned the novel down. Vladimir Dimitrijevic – a Serb working for the publishers *L'Age d'Homme* in Lausanne – eventually accepted the novel and in 1980 published an almost-complete Russian text. At a conference about Vasily Grossman in 2003 in Turin, Dimitrijevic said he had sensed at once that Grossman was portraying 'a world in three dimensions' and that he was one of those rare writers whose aim was 'not to prove something but to make people live something.'

Grossman, however, did not live to see any of this; he did not know that his manuscripts would be preserved, let alone be published. According to Lipkin: 'Grossman aged before our eyes. His curly hair turned greyer and a bald patch appeared. His asthma [...] returned. His walk became a shuffle.'[6] Grossman himself said, 'They strangled me in a dark corner.'[7]

Tatiana Menaker has provided us with another glimpse of Grossman during these years – although the first of her memories, in fact, dates back to 1959, two years before the 'arrest' of *Life and Fate*: 'A mysterious stone wall of unsaid things and secrecy always surrounded him. My first memory of this sadness and secrecy belongs to the year 1959, when I spent a winter vacation in Viktor Sherentsis' house in Moscow. Grossman came to visit every day and I was constantly being kicked out into the corridor stuffed with books. No wonder: as my grandma was always repeating, "Even the cat reports to the OGPU."[8] I knew that Grossman was a famous writer. We had his huge novels, which were published in millions of copies, but the aura of sadness and tragedy was never explained to me in his lifetime. Later I realized that the people who came to our apartment had been sharing with Grossman their prison camp memories. I vividly recall that I felt in their presence the truth of Grossman's observation that these people are "frozen in time".'[9]

From late 1961 Grossman was often seriously ill. He did not realize this, but he was suffering from the first stages of cancer. A doctor ascribed his symptoms to eating too much spicy food during his journey to Armenia in November and December 1961. Lipkin also remembers Grossman telling him in late 1962 that there was blood in his urine; he seems to have failed to act on a doctor's advice to visit a urologist.[10] In May 1963 Grossman underwent an operation to remove one of his kidneys – the initial site of his cancer.

Late on 14 September, 1964, after a period of several months in hospital, Grossman died of lung cancer.[11]

[1] Guber, *op. cit.*, p. 99

[2] Most published sources refer to this woman as Lyolya Dominikina. Korotkova has explained the origin of this confusion. Korotkova remembers Lyolya Klestova as one of the four people – together with herself, Zabolotskaya and Grossman – who attended the funeral of Grossman's father in 1956. Some time after Grossman's death, Zabolotskaya told Korotkova that it was Klestova who had preserved the manuscript of *Life and Fate*, in a communal apartment, in a locked suitcase under her bed. Critics and journalists writing about Grossman knew from Zabolotskaya and Korotkova that the manuscript has been preserved by a woman called 'Lyolya', but they confused this Lyolya with another Lyolya, the niece (or possibly daughter from a previous marriage) of a family friend by the name of Dominika who had at one time been married to Grossman's father. In his letters, however, Grossman refers to this other Lyolya not as 'Lyolya Dominikina', but as 'Dominika's Lyolya' (*Dominikina Lyolya*). No-one by the name of Lyolya Dominikina ever existed. Symbolically, however, it seems appropriate that the preservation of Grossman's manuscript should be ascribed to a mythical figure. See also Korotkova 'O moem otse', p. 48]

[3] The OGPU confiscated two copies of the manuscript of *The Heart of a Dog* from Mikhail Bulgakov's flat in May 1926; two years later, however, these were returned. A comparison of the authorities' treatment of *Life and Fate* with their treatment of *Doctor Zhivago* is revealing. Pasternak showed *Doctor Zhivago* to friends and editors and even trusted the manuscript to the Soviet postal service; his offence lay not in writing the novel but in publishing it abroad.

[4] Before his death Grossman arranged for Klestova to give her copy to another old friend, Vyacheslav Loboda, who lived in a town about 150 kilometres from Moscow. In 1988 Loboda's widow gave this copy to Fyodor Guber and it was used to correct textual lacunae before the text established by Etkind and Markish was republished in Russia.

[5] 'Posvyashchayetsya Vasiliyu Grossmanu' in *Narod moy*, number 18, 30 Sept, 2007; also at http://www.jew.spb.ru/ami/A406/A406-041.html]

[6] Lipkin, *op. cit.*, p. 582

[7] *ibid*, p. 575

[8] *Koshka sluzhit v GPU.*

[9] Email message from Tatiana Menaker. Korotkova suggests that Menaker's sense of Grossman's tension and sadness can, at least in part, be accounted for by a tension (which Korotkova herself learned about only long after Grossman's death) between Grossman and Viktor Sherentsis. Her own memories of her father are very different.

[10] Lipkin, *op. cit.*, p. 615

[11] According to Korotkova, John and Carol Garrard are mistaken in ascribing Grossman's death to stomach cancer.

Bibliography of Lipkin's Work

Poetry:

Ochevidets [Eyewitness: poems of various years]. Elista: Kalmyk Book Publishers, 1967; 2nd Edition, 1974

Vechnyi Den' [Eternal Day]. Moscow: Sovetskii Pisatel, 1975

Volia [Free Will]; selected by Joseph Brodsky. Ann Arbor: Ardis, 1981; Moscow: O.G.I., 2003.

Kochevoi Ogon' [A Nomadic Flame]. Ann Arbor: Ardis, 1984

Kartiny i golosa [Pictures and Voices]. London: Overseas Publications Interchange, 1986

Lira. Stikhi Raznyh Let [Lyre. Verses of Various Years]. Moscow: Pravda, 1989

Lunnyi Svet. Stikhotvoreniya i Poemy [Moonlight. Verses and Poems]. Moscow: Sovremennik, 1991

Pis'mena. Stikhotvoreniya i Poemy [Letters. Verses and Poems]. Moscow: Khudozhestvennaia Literatura, 1991

Pered Zakhodom Solntsa. Stikhi i Perevody [Before the Sunset. Verses and Translations] Paris-Moscow-New York: Tretya Volna, 1995

Posokh [Shepherd's Crook]. Moscow: CheRo, 1997

Sobranie sochinenia v 4-kh tomakh [Collected works in 4 volumes]. Moscow: Vagrius, 1998

Sem' desiatiletii [Seven Decades]. Moscow: Vozvrashchenie, 2000

Vmeste. Stikhi [Together, Verses. (Together with Inna Lisnyanskaya)]. Moscow: Grail, Russkiy put', 2000

Ochevidets [Eyewitness: selected poems]; compiled by Inna Lisnianskaya. Moscow: Vremia, 2008

English translations of Semyon Lipkin's work

Four poems translated by Albert C. Todd, in Twentieth Century Russian Poetry, selected with an introduction by Yevgeny Yevtushenko, edited by Albert C. Todd and Max Hayward, with Daniel Weissbort. New York: Doubleday; London: Fourth Estate, 1993.

Semyon Lipkin's Prose:

The Stalingrad Ship, stories 1943

Decade – (first novel) 1983

Stalingrad of Vasily Grossman 1984

Life and Fate of Vasily Grossman. Farewell (With Anna Berzer) 1990

The Flaming Coal. Sketches and Discourses, 1991

The Second Road (memoirs) 1995

Blazing Fire (sketches and observations about Georgii Shengeli) 1995

Quadriga (short fiction and memoirs) 1997

Examples of Translations by Semyon Lipkin:

Abkhaz

Bagrat Shikuba, Moi zemlyaki [My Compatriots, a poem]; transl. from Abkhaz by S. Lipkin and Ya. Kozlovsky. Moscow, 1967.

Akkadian

Gilgamesh; verse adaptation by Semyon Lipkin; afterword by Vyacheslav V. Ivanov. St Petersburg: Pushkin Fund, 2001.

Buryat

Geser [Geser, Buryat Heroic Epos]; Moscow: Khudozhestvennaia Literatura, 1968

Derzhava rannikh zhavoronkov. Povest po motivam buryatskogo eposa [The State of Early Skylarks. A novella on the Motives of Buryat Epos]; a children's version by S. Lipkin. Moscow: Detgiz, 1968.

Dagestani

Dagestanskie liriki [Dagestani Lyric Poets]; translations by S.I. Lipkin and others. Leningrad: Sovetskii Pisatel', 1961.

Kabardian

Shogentsukov, Ali. Poemy [Poems]; translated from Kabardian by Semyon Lipkin. Moscow: Sovetskii Pisatel', 1949.

Narty [Narts, Kabardian Epos]; translated by Semyon Lipkin. Moscow: Khudozhestvennaia Literatura, 1951.

Kabardinskaia epicheskaya poezia [Kabardian Epic Poetry]; selected translations. Nal'chik, 1956.

Debet Zlatolikii i ego druzia: Balkaro-Karachaev nartskii epos [Debet Goldenface and his friends: Karachai-Balkar Nart epic]; translated by S. Lipkin. Nal'chik: Elbrus, 1973.

Kalmyk

Prikliyucheniya bogatyrya Samshura, prozvannogo Lotosom [Adventures of Hero Shamshur, Nicknamed Lotus], a children's adaptation of the Kalmyk epic story by Semyon Lipkin. Moscow: Detgiz, 1958.

Dzhangar: Kalmytski narodny epos [Djangar: Kalmyk national epic]; translated by Semyon Lipkin. Elista: Kalmyk Book Publishers, 1971, repr. 1977.

Dzhangar: Kalmytski narodny epos; novye pesni [Djangar: Kalmyk national epic; new songs]; poetic translations realised by V.N. Eremenko, S.I. Lipkin, Yu. M. Neiman. Elista: Kalmyk Book Publishers, 1990.

Kirghiz

Kirgizskii narodnyi epos "Manas" [Kirghiz Folk Epos Manas], transl. Semyon Lipkin and Mark Tarlovsky. Moscow: Khudozhestvennaia Literatura, 1941.

Poety Kirgizii: Stikhi 1941-1944 [Kirghiz Poets: Verses 1941-1944]; translated under the editorship of S. Lipkin. Moscow: Sovetskiy Pisatel', 1946.

Manas Velikodushny: povest [Manas the Magnanimous: a novella]; [version by S. Lipkin]. Leningrad, 1947.

Manas: epizody iz kirgizskogo narodnogo eposa [Manas: episodes from the Kirghiz national epic]; translated by S. Lipkin and L. Penkovski. Moscow: Khudozhestvennaia Literatura, 1960.

Manas Velikodushny. Povest' o drevnikh kirghizskikh geroyakh [Manas the Magnanimous: a Story about Ancient Kirghiz Heroes]; Riga: Polaris, 1995.

Sanskrit

Mahabharata (Indian epic). In: series Biblioteka vsemirnoi literatury, vol. 2, translated from Sanskrit by S. Lipkin. Moscow: Khudozhestvennaia Literatura, 1969.

Tatar

Poety Tatarii, 1941-1944 [Poets of Tataria, 1941-1944]; edited by A. Erikeeva and S. Lipkin. Moscow: Sovetskii Pisatel', 1945.

Poeziya Sovetskoi Tatarii: Sbornik sostavlen Soiuzom Sovetskikh Pisatelei Tatarskoi ASSR [Poetry of Soviet Tataria: Collection compiled by the Union of Soviet Tatar Writers]; editor S.I. Lipkin [translations by various hands]. Moscow: Khudozhestvennaia Literatura, 1955.

Idegei: tatarskii narodnyi epos [Idegei: Tatar national epic]; translated by Semyon Lipkin. Kazan': Tatar Book Publishers, 1990.

Tadjik-Farsi

Firdawsi. Skazanie o Bakhrame Chubine [Epos about Bakhram Chubin], a fragment from poem Shāhnāmah translated from Tadjik-Farsi by S. Lipkin. Stalinabad [Dushanbe]: Tadzhikgosizdat, 1952.

Izbrannoe [Selections]; translated from Tadjik-Farsi by V. Levik and S. Lipkin. Moscow, 1957.

Firdawsi. Poėmy iz Shakh-namė [Poems from Shāhnāmah]; in translation by S. Lipkin. Stalinabad [Dushanbe]: Tadzhikgosizdat, 1959.

Stranitsy Tadzhikskoy Poezii [Pages of Tadjik Poetry], ed. S. Lipkin, Stalinabad [Dushanbe]: Tadzikgosizdat, 1961.

Rudaki, stikhi [Rudaki, verses], transl. S. Lipkin and V. Levik, ed. I. Braginsky. Moscow: Nauka, 1964.

Tetrad' bytiia [Book of Life]; Poetry in Tadjik dialect with Russian by Semyon Lipkin. Lipkin. Dushanbe: Irfon, 1977.

Uzbek

Khamid Alimdzhan. Oigul i Bakhtiyor [Oigul i Bakhtiyor]; Tashkent: Goslitizdat UzSSR, 1948.

Lutfi. Gul I Navruz [Gul and Navruz, a poem]; transl. S.Lipkin. Tashkent: Goslitizdat UzSSR, 1959.

Navoi, Leili i Medzhnun [Leili and Medjnun]; poem translated from Uzbek by Semyon Lipkin. Moscow: Goslitizdat, 1945; Moscow: Detgiz, 1948; Tashkent: Khudozhestvennaia Literatura, 1957; (In: A. Navoi. Poemy [Poems].), Moscow: Khudozhestvennaia Literatura, 1972.

Navoi, Sem' Planet [Seven Planets]; poem translated from Uzbek by

Semyon Lipkin. Tashkent, 1948; Moscow, 1954; (In: A. Navoi. Poemy [Poems].), Moscow: Khudozhestvennaia Literatura, 1972.

Golosa Shesti Stoletii [Voices of Six Centuries]; selected translations from Uzbek. Tashkent, 1960.

Tsarevna iz goroda T'my [Princess from the City of Darkness]; children's story by S. Lipkin based on Uzbek tales. Moscow: Detgiz, 1961.

Slovo i Kamen [Word and Stone], selected translations from Uzbek poetry by S. Lipkin, Tashkent: Gafur Gulyam Publ., 1977.

Various languages

Stroki Mudrykh [Lines of the Wise Ones], coll. translations by S. Lipkin, Moscow: Sovetskiy Pisatel', 1961.

O bogatyriakh, umeltsakh i volshebnikhakh [On Heroes, Craftsmen and Wizards]; 3 novellas on Caucasian folklore motives, children's adaptation by S. Lipkin. Moscow: Detgiz, 1963.

Zolotaya zep' [The Golden Chain: Eastern Poems]; translated from Abkhaz, Tadzhik-Farsi, old-Uzbek, etc. Moscow: Detgiz, 1970.

Dalekie i Blizkie: Stikhi zarubezhnykh poetov v perevode [Far and Near: Verses by foreign poets in translation]; translators: Vera Markova, Semyon Lipkin, Aleksandr Gitovich. Moscow: Progress, 1978.

Bibliography of other works referred to:

Life and Fate – Vasily Grossman – Vintage Classics 2011

The Return – Andrey Platonov – The Harvill Press 1999

Happy Moscow – Andrey Platonov tr. Robert and Elizabeth Chandler, London: Harvill, 2001

A Writer at War – Vasily Grossman ed. Beever and Vinogradova London: Pimlico, 2006

Soul and Other Stories – Andrey Platonov tr. Robert and Elizabeth Chandler et al. New York: NYRB Classics, 2007

The Foundation Pit – Andrey Platonov tr. Robert and Elizabeth Chandler and Olga Meerson, London: Vintage Classics, 2010

The Road – Vasily Grossman tr. Robert and Elizabeth Chandler, London: Maclehose Press, 2010

Notes

To Inna p23
Inna – The poet Inna Lisnianskaya, Lipkin's wife. Her father was Jewish and her mother was an Armenian Christian. Inna was baptized by her *nyanya* and considers herself a Christian.

Anthem p25
Derzhavin – 18th century poet who wrote classical anthems commemorating Russian victories over the Ottomans.

Mikhael p29
Mikhael – Semyon Lipkin's brother who died in 1990.

Stopped p33
The *Old Testament* laws given to Noah for the civilization of mankind after the flood include a prohibition against eating flesh cut from live animals, Genesis 9:4.

Moldavian is a Language p36
Vorkuta – town inside the arctic circle built by slave labour . Mamalyga – porridge.

Verlaine p51
This is Lipkin's version of Paul Verlaine's *Sagesse [Wisdom]*.

The Covenant p55
Covenant – Genesis 15:17.

Ye of Little Faith p59
Ye of little faith – Luke 12:27–38 / Mathew 8:25-26/14:30–31.

Bliss p61
Stanistas – villages. Chirchir – young wine.

Winter Sunset at the Diner P71
I'm indebted to Poel Karp who confirms that Lipkin met Tsvetaeva in the U.S.S.R. after she came back in 1939 to follow her husband, Sergey Efron and their daughter, Ariadna. In October 1939 the Soviets arrested Efron and shot him in August 1941.

Sandomirsky's brave daughter:- Sandomirsky Voevoda was the commander in Pushkin's *Boris Godunov*. Marina Mnishek was *Sandomirsky's daughter.* Lipkin defines Tsvetaeva in terms used by Pushkin, whom she so admired, but he introduces the word, *brave,* to pay his own homage to the way Tsvetaeva identified with both her namesake's courageous lineage and uncompromising national pride.

The Moskva is Moscow's river, alongside which the main streets were Sovietised by 1939 but the walk in the second stanza describes the backstreets Tsvetaeva knew before she left Russia in 1922

Myshkin – Prince Myshkin another tragic returnee, in Dostoyevsky's *The Idiot.*

Merezhkovsky (1865–1941) – writer and philosopher and Balmont (1867–1942) poets who had both left Russia by 1920.

Elabuga and that Tartar rope – On 31st August 1941 Tsvetaeva hanged herself in Elabuga on the river Kama in Tatarstan.

The Rose of Yerevan p75
Yerevan – Capital of Armenia.

The Cossack Mother p77
Lipkin saw the Sistine Madonna when it was exhibited in Moscow in 1955, by the Soviet Government, prior to its return along with that of other paintings removed from the Dresden Art Gallery after the German defeat.

In the Tian Shan p81
Tian Shan – mountains in central Asia. Kumgan – a narrow mouthed, lidded, single-handled ewer. RAYFO – Rayonny Finansovy Otdel, the district's financial department.

Smith/Doorstop Books, Pamphlets and Audio

25 years

of titles by

Moniza Alvi, Simon Armitage, Jane Aspinall, Ann Atkinson, Sally Baker, Mike Barlow, Kate Bass, Suzanne Batty, Chris Beckett, Catherine Benson, Gerard Benson, Sujata Bhatt, Nina Boyd, Sue Boyle, Susan Bright, Carole Bromley, Sue Butler, Liz Cashdan, Dennis Casling, Julia Casterton, Clare Chapman, Linda Chase, Debjani Chatterjee, Stanley Cook, Bob Cooper, Jennifer Copley, Paula Cunningham, Simon Currie, Duncan Curry, Peter Daniels, Jonathan Davidson, Kwame Dawes, Julia Deakin, Steve Dearden, Patricia Debney, Tim Dooley, Jane Draycott, Carol Ann Duffy, Sue Dymoke, Nell Farrell, Catherine Fisher, Janet Fisher, Sam Gardiner, Adele Geras, Sally Goldsmith, Yvonne Green, Harry Guest, Robert Hamberger, Sophie Hannah, John Harvey, Jo Haslam, Geoff Hattersley, Jeanette Hattersley, Marko Hautala, Selima Hill, Andrea Holland, Sian Hughes, Keith Jafrate, Lesley Jeffries, Chris Jones, Mimi Khalvati, John Killick, Stephen Knight, Judith Lal, John Lancaster, Peter Lane, Michael Laskey, Brenda Lealman, Tim Liardet, John Lyons, Cheryl Martin, Eleanor Maxted, Michael McCarthy, John McAuliffe, Patrick McGuinness, Kath Mckay, Paul McLoughlin, Hugh McMillan, Ian McMillan, Allison McVety, Hilary Menos, Paul Mills, Hubert Moore, David Morley, Paul Munden, Sean O'Brien, Padraig O'Morain, Les Murray, Stephanie Norgate, Christopher North, Dorothy Nimmo, Carita Nystrom, Alan Payne, Pascale Petit, Ann Pilling, Mike Di Placido, Jim Pollard, Simon Rae, Irene Rawnsley, Ed Reiss, Padraig Rooney, Jane Routh, Michael Schmidt, Myra Schneider, Ted Schofield, Kathryn Simmonds, Lemn Sissay, Felicity Skelton, Catherine Smith, Elspeth Smith, Joan Jobe Smith, Cherry Smyth, Pauline Stainer, Martin Stannard, Adam Strickson, Mandy Sutter Diana Syder, Pam Thompson, Susan Utting, Steven Waling, Martyn Wiley, Andrew Wilson, River Wolton, Sue Wood, Anna Woodford, Mary Woodward, Cliff Yates …

www.poetrybusiness.co.uk